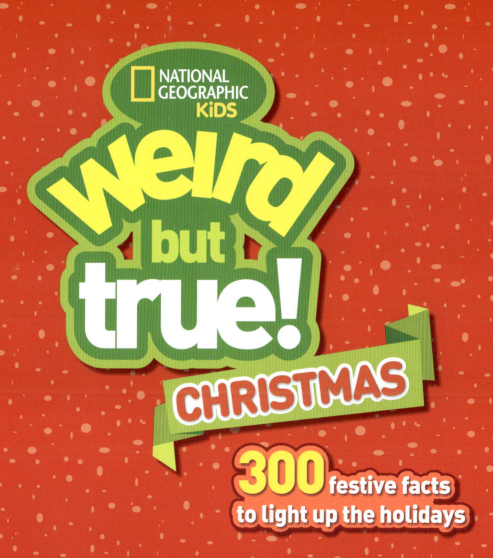

IT'S NOT JUST A WINTER MYTH! YOUR TONGUE REALLY CAN GET STUCK TO A PIECE OF FROZEN METAL.

Don't try this at home!

A Canadian scientist built a machine that grows icicles.

A business magazine once listed SANTA as one of the WORLD'S RICHEST PEOPLE.

4

THE PINE NEEDLES ON SOME CHRISTMAS TREES ARE EDIBLE.

Do not eat any leaves without an adult's guidance.

The world's **longest** CHRISTMAS LIST stretched **13,053** feet (3,979 m) and took **1 hour** and **40 minutes** to be unrolled.

THE BERRIES OF SOME MISTLETOE PLANTS EXPLODE.

"The Christmas Song (CHESTNUTS ROASTING ON AN OPEN FIRE)" was written during a summer heat wave.

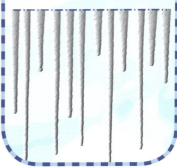

YOU ARE MORE LIKELY TO FIND **ICICLES HANGING** ON THE **SOUTH SIDE** OF A BUILDING THAN THE **NORTH SIDE.**

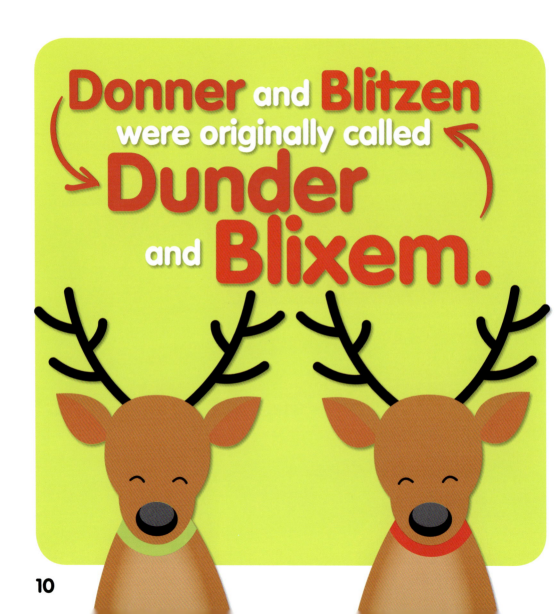

PEOPLE IN PARTS OF SOUTH AFRICA SNACK ON **DEEP-FRIED CATERPILLARS** ON CHRISTMAS DAY.

There is EGGNOG-flavored lip balm.

IN INDIA, PEOPLE DECORATE BANANA TREES FOR CHRISTMAS.

11

OF ADULT REINDEER, ONLY FEMALES KEEP THEIR ANTLERS THROUGH DECEMBER. (THAT MEANS SANTA'S REINDEER ARE PROBABLY ALL GIRLS!)

THE HIGHEST-ALTITUDE Christmas carol concert WAS PERFORMED ON AN AIRPLANE AT 39,000 FEET. (11,887 m)

BRAVO!

Some of the **first toboggans** were made from **whale bone.**

WHAT SANTA CLAUS IS CALLED...

in Russia: **Ded Moroz**

in Germany: **Weihnachtsmann**

in South Korea: **Santa Kollosu**

in Brazil: **Papai Noel**

in South Africa: **Vader Kersfees**

in Australia and New Zealand: **Father Christmas**

Italian children look out for **Befana,** a friendly witch who comes down the chimney to bring candy and toys on Christmas.

Sugarplums DO NOT CONTAIN PLUMS— they're SEEDS or NUTS dipped in SUGAR.

EVERY SNOWFLAKE HAS SIX SIDES.

17

AN OFFICIAL GOVERNMENT WEBSITE TRACKS **THE MOVEMENT OF SANTA'S SLEIGH ON CHRISTMAS EVE**

As a prank, Apollo astronauts once **radioed NASA** that they had seen a **UFO piloted** by someone in **A RED SUIT.**

FAR OUT!

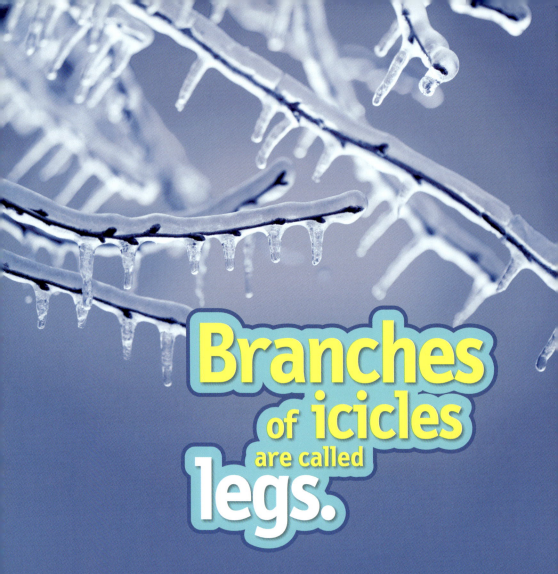

Branches of icicles are called legs.

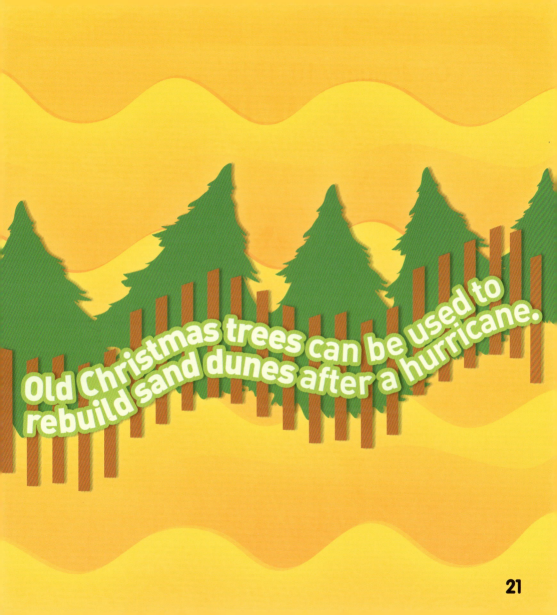

The snowflake moray eel has two jaws to help it snatch its prey.

THE UNITED STATES GROWS **MORE THAN**

Cook County, Illinois, U.S.A., uses old Christmas trees to build habitats for wild animals.

ASPIRING MALL SANTAS CAN LEARN THE JOB AT THE INTERNATIONAL UNIVERSITY OF **SANTA CLAUS.**

40 MILLION POINSETTIAS EVERY YEAR.

U.S. PRESIDENT THEODORE ROOSEVELT BANNED CHRISTMAS TREES FROM THE WHITE HOUSE.

Good King Wenceslas was a real ruler in medieval Bohemia.

Candy canes started off as straight white sticks.

28

Some scholars think that Jesus may have actually been born in the spring.

An American woman set the **record** for the most **Christmas trees** chopped down in two minutes: **27.**

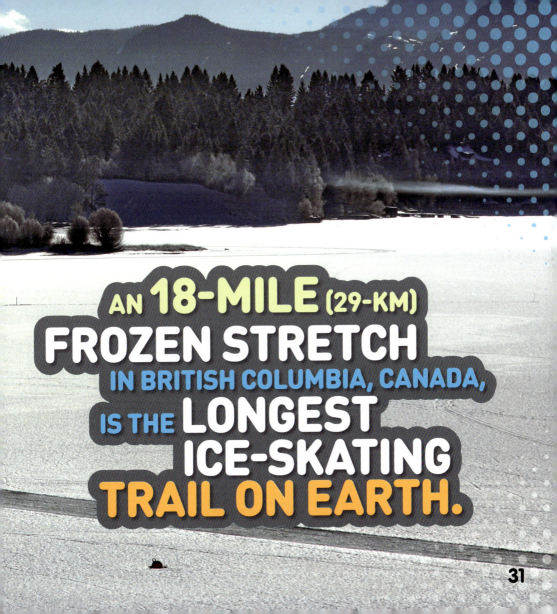

U.S. STORES MAKE MORE THAN $600 BILLION IN SALES DURING THE HOLIDAY SEASON.

PEOPLE BUY LESS WHEN A STORE'S MUSIC IS LOUD.

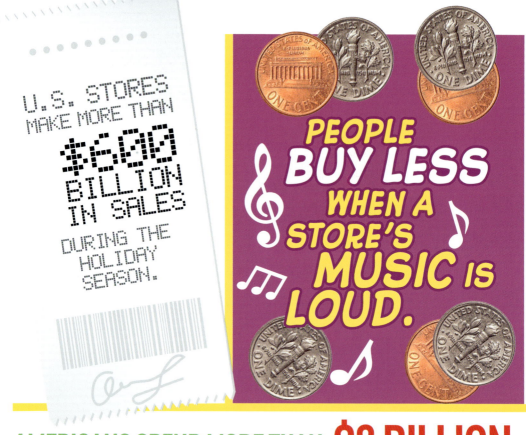

AMERICANS SPEND MORE THAN $2 BILLION

A *170-year-old* hand-colored Christmas card once sold at auction for nearly **$30,000.**

A YEAR ON WRAPPING PAPER.

SNOW SOMETIMES APPEARS BLUE.

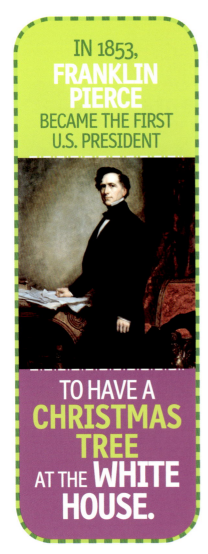

IN 1853, **FRANKLIN PIERCE** BECAME THE FIRST U.S. PRESIDENT TO HAVE A **CHRISTMAS TREE** AT THE **WHITE HOUSE.**

On Christmas Eve in Norway, some families hide their **brooms** so that **evil witches** won't steal them **overnight.**

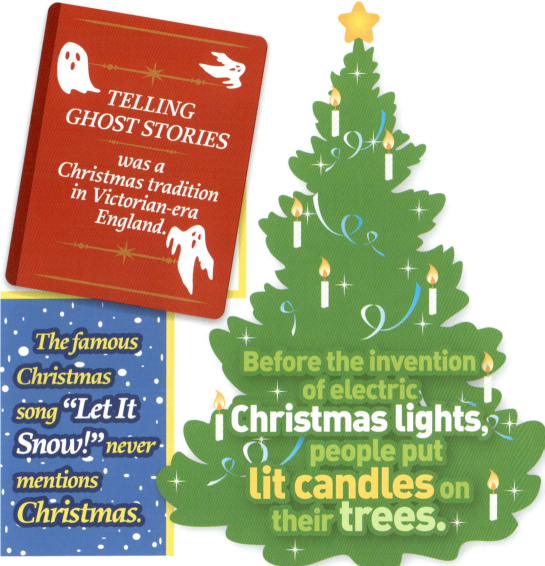

TELLING GHOST STORIES *was a Christmas tradition in Victorian-era England.*

The famous Christmas song "Let It Snow!" never mentions Christmas.

Before the invention of electric Christmas lights, people put lit candles on their trees.

Each Christmas, a building in California, U.S.A., is topped with a red bow that's as wide as a tennis court.

THERE ARE 1,300 SPECIES OF MISTLETOE.

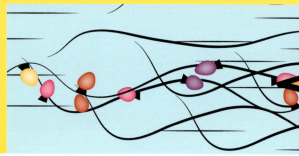

IN BRAZIL, FAMILIES DECORATE PINE TREES WITH LITTLE PIECES OF COTTON TO REPRESENT FALLING SNOW.

The average person spends a total of **19** hours CHRISTMAS SHOPPING EACH YEAR.

IF YOU WERE FLYING SANTA'S SLEIGH, YOU'D HAVE TO TRAVEL 1,280 MILES (2,060 km/s) PER SECOND TO REACH EVERYONE IN TIME.

THE WORLD'S LARGEST GINGERBREAD HOUSE WAS A TWO-STORY HOME.

IT WAS MADE WITH:

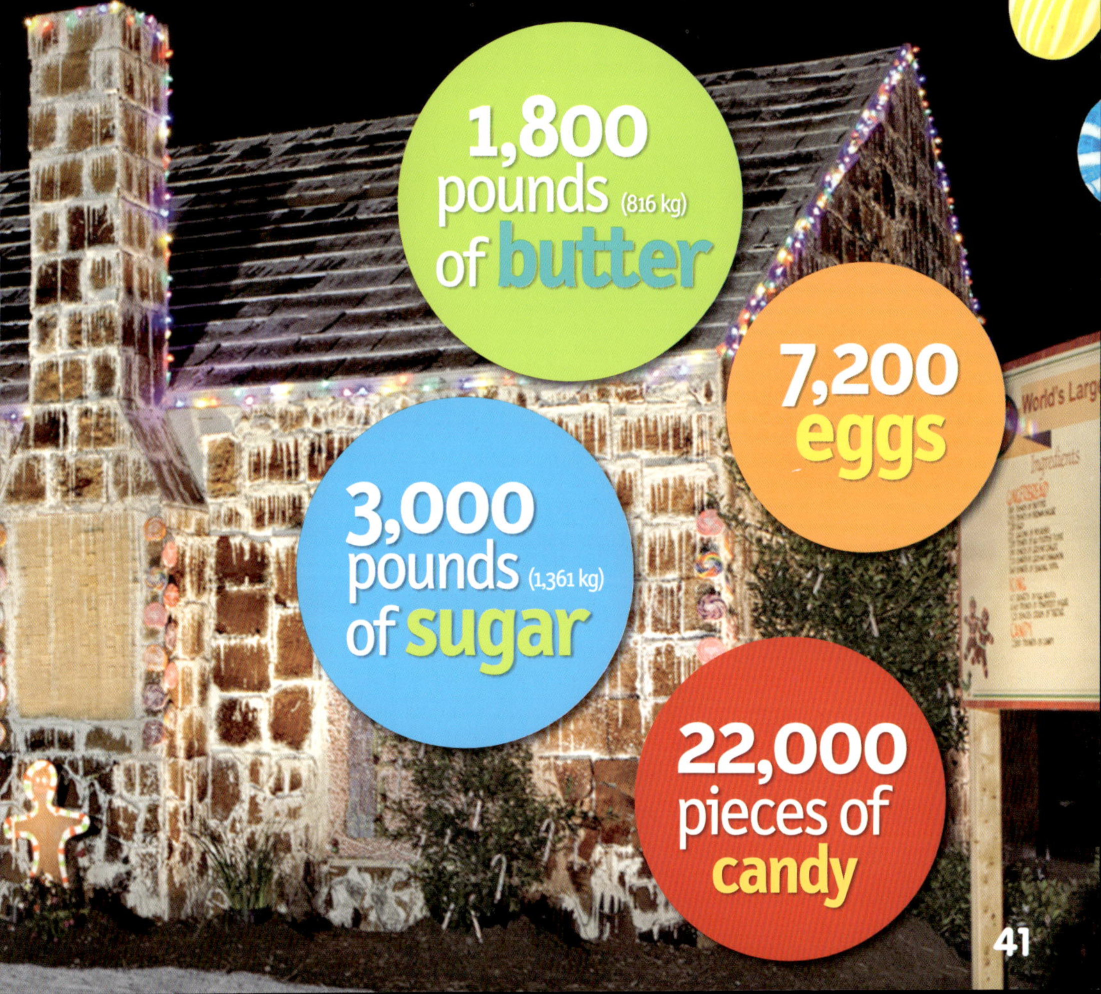

1,800 pounds (816 kg) **of butter**

7,200 eggs

3,000 pounds (1,361 kg) **of sugar**

22,000 pieces of candy

41

SCIENTISTS AT THE NORTH POLE WORK ON FLOATING RESEARCH STATIONS.

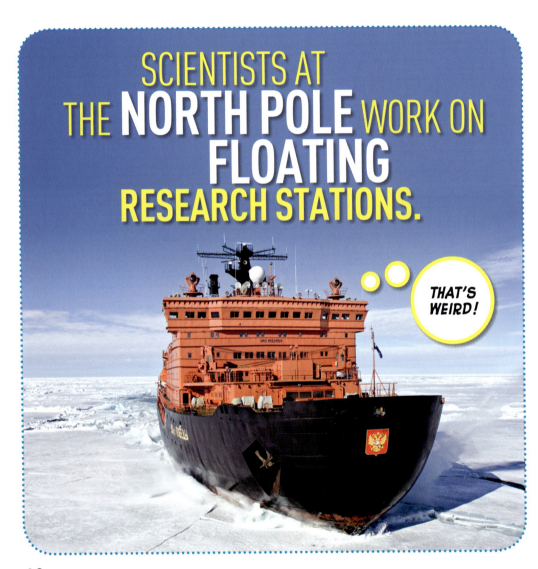

THAT'S WEIRD!

Factories in Shijiao, China, recycle discarded Christmas lights into slipper soles.

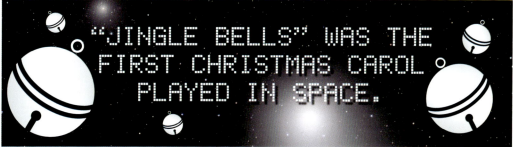

"JINGLE BELLS" WAS THE FIRST CHRISTMAS CAROL PLAYED IN SPACE.

THE 12 DAYS OF CHRISTMAS ACTUALLY COME AFTER CHRISTMAS.

In medieval times, holiday revelers feasted on stuffed peacocks and boar meat.

A Canadian man has a collection of more than 25,000 items featuring Santa Claus.

A HOTEL IN DUBAI, UNITED ARAB EMIRATES, **DISPLAYED** A CHRISTMAS TREE COVERED IN **181 PIECES** OF JEWELRY VALUED AT MORE THAN **$11 MILLION.**

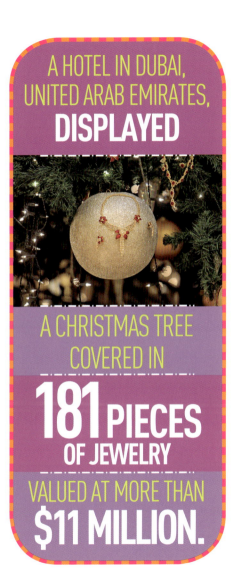

People in the United Kingdom traditionally **bake coins, buttons, thimbles,** *or* **wishbones** *into Christmas desserts.*

Early **SLEDS** were discovered on an excavated **VIKING SHIP.**

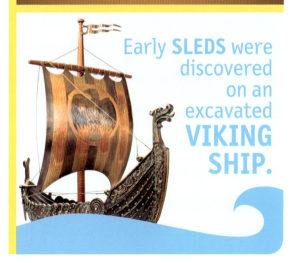

49

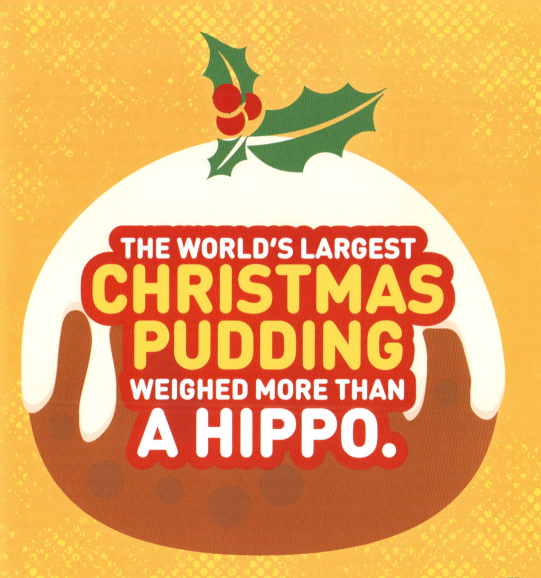

IN BRITAIN, EATING A **MINCE PIE** FOR EACH OF THE **12 DAYS** OF **CHRISTMAS** IS SAID TO BRING **GOOD LUCK.**

Some scientists are trying to **clone evergreens** to create the **perfect Christmas tree.**

52

PARTICIPANTS IN THE WORLD'S LARGEST GATHERING OF PEOPLE DRESSED LIKE CHRISTMAS ELVES

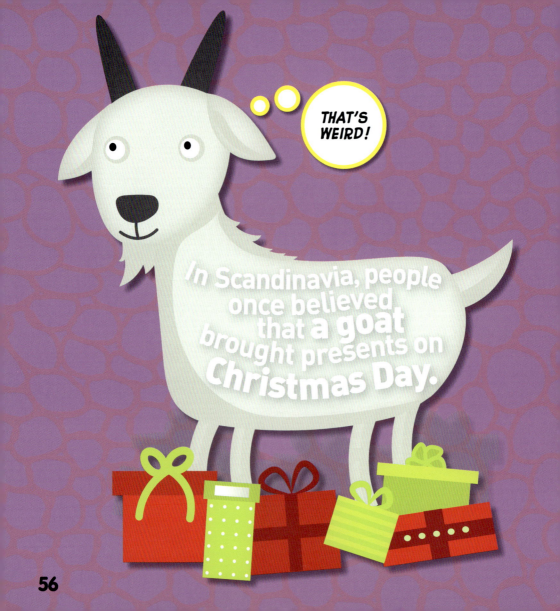

The earliest Christmas trees—dating back to 1510—were decorated with apples and paper roses.

Visitors to a museum in Virginia, U.S.A., can perform experiments on **holiday fruitcake.**

Tinsel was once made out of thin pieces of real silver.

35,000 BASEBALL FANS BROKE THE **WORLD RECORD** FOR THE LARGEST GATHERING OF PEOPLE WEARING **SANTA HATS.**

Kids in Iceland fear **the Yule Cat,** *a mythical monster who is said to eat children at Christmastime.*

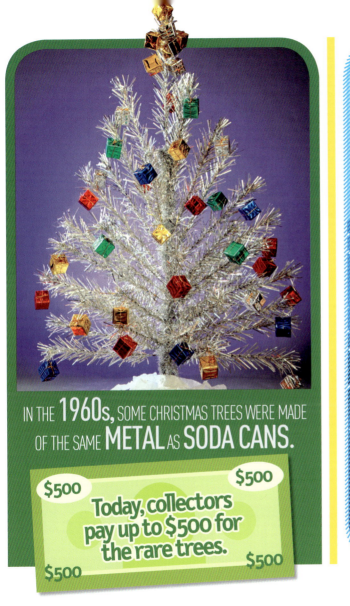

IN THE **1960s**, SOME CHRISTMAS TREES WERE MADE OF THE SAME **METAL** AS **SODA CANS**.

Today, collectors pay up to $500 for the rare trees.

A SINGLE SNOWSTORM CAN DROP **40 MILLION TONS** (36.3 million t) OF SNOW.

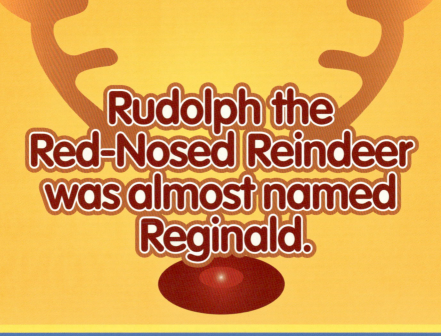

Rudolph the Red-Nosed Reindeer was almost named Reginald.

364 = the total number of gifts given in the song "The Twelve Days of Christmas"

Mathematicians study how fast checkout lines move when people are Christmas shopping.

IS IT HOT IN HERE?

AT AN ANNUAL FESTIVAL IN ZURICH, SWITZERLAND, PEOPLE BLOW UP A GIANT SNOWMAN FILLED WITH FIREWORKS.

67

ONE OF THE WORLD'S **TALLEST LIVING** CHRISTMAS TREES—A **162-FOOT** (4.9-m) FIR IN IDAHO, U.S.A.—IS DECORATED WITH MORE THAN **TWO MILES** (3.2 km) OF LIGHTS EACH YEAR.

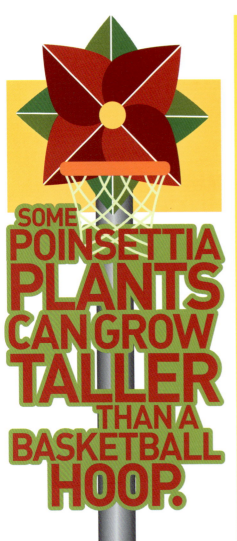

FRIED CHICKEN IS THE **MOST POPULAR CHRISTMAS EVE MEAL** IN JAPAN.

National Candy Cane Day is celebrated on December 26 in the United States.

The 1946 Christmas classic *It's a Wonderful Life* used a combination of soap and a fire-fighting chemical to make fake movie snow.

"Snow" was once made on movie sets by painting cornflakes white.

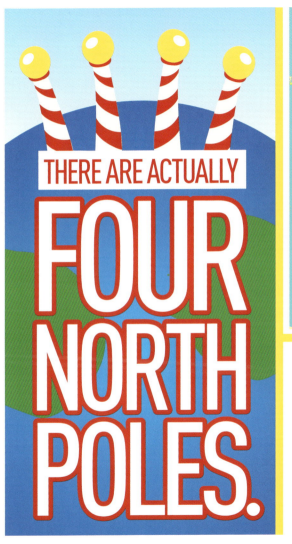

THERE ARE ACTUALLY **FOUR NORTH POLES.**

Christmas caroling began as *"wassailing,"* an Old English custom of *greeting* and *toasting friends.*

U.S. president Andrew Jackson once held an **indoor** snowball fight at the **White House.**

73

The fastest time for a marathoner in **A GINGERBREAD MAN** costume is **3 HOURS 29 MINUTES.**

75

The world's largest **CHRISTMAS STOCKING** measures as long as **FOUR SCHOOL BUSES** lined up end to end.

A TEAM OF SCIENTISTS IN THE UNITED KINGDOM CREATED CHRISTMAS CARDS SO TINY THAT **8,276** OF THEM WOULD FIT ON JUST ONE POSTAGE STAMP.

12 percent of Earth's surface is permanently covered in ice and snow.

The world's **largest wreath** was wider than a soccer field and heavier than **two elephants.**

IN UKRAINE, **PEOPLE DECORATE** THEIR CHRISTMAS TREES WITH **FAKE SPIDERS AND WEBS.**

THE LARGEST CUP OF HOT CHOCOLATE EVER MADE COULD HAVE FILLED 20 BATHTUBS.

TUDOR CHRISTMAS PIE =
a **pigeon** inside
a **partridge** inside
a **chicken** inside
a **goose** inside
a **turkey** inside
a **pie** crust

One snowflake can contain 180 billion molecules of water.

QUEEN ELIZABETH I *had a baker create* **LIFE-SIZE GINGERBREAD COOKIE MODELS** *of her important* **ROYAL GUESTS.**

THE LARGEST GATHERING OF PEOPLE WEARING HOLIDAY-THEMED SWEATERS: 3,473 PEOPLE, AT A BASKETBALL GAME IN KANSAS, U.S.A.

IN FLORIDA, U.S.A., PEOPLE MAKE SNOWMEN OUT OF SAND.

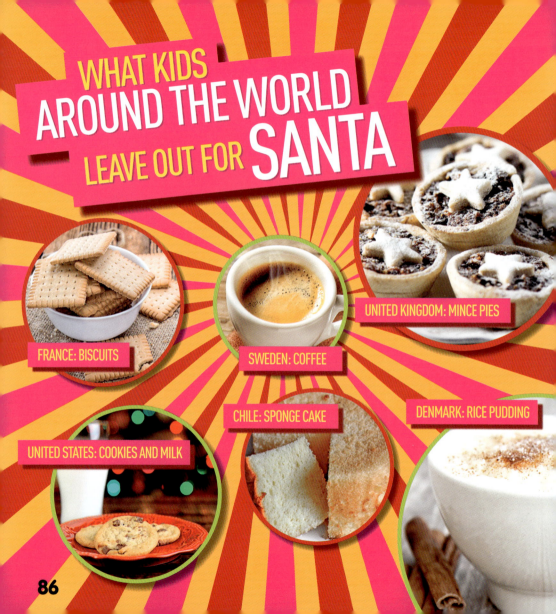

The state song of Maryland, U.S.A., is sung to the tune of "O Christmas Tree."

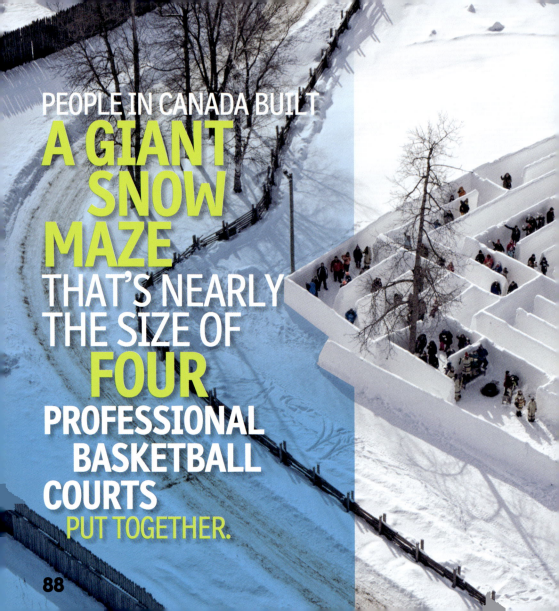

PEOPLE IN CANADA BUILT **A GIANT SNOW MAZE** THAT'S NEARLY THE SIZE OF **FOUR** PROFESSIONAL BASKETBALL COURTS PUT TOGETHER.

A man legally named **Santa Claus** was elected to the city council of North Pole, Alaska, U.S.A., in 2015.

THE TOWN GÄVLE, SWEDEN, **ERECTS A GIANT STRAW GOAT AT CHRISTMAS.**

THE YULE GOAT HAS ITS

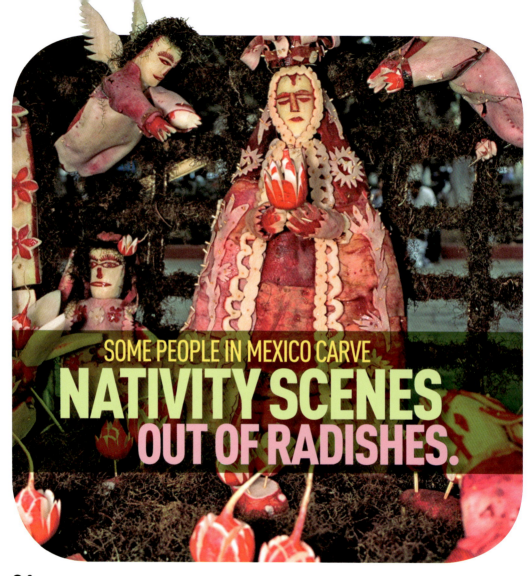

According to one calculation, **Santa's sleigh weighs around 700 million pounds.**

(317.5 million kg)

CHRISTMAS DINNER ABOARD THE INTERNATIONAL SPACE STATION HAS INCLUDED TURKEY AND POTATOES IN PLASTIC POUCHES.

ASTRONAUTS ON AN AMERICAN SPACE STATION ONCE

MADE A CHRISTMAS TREE OUT OF FOOD CANS.

It takes up to 10 years to grow a Christmas tree.

EACH YEAR, PEOPLE IN THE UNITED STATES SPEND SOME $1.6 BILLION ON HOLIDAY CANDY.

AMERICANS PREFER chocolate Santas to chocolate snowmen, according to a recent survey.

A whole **sheep's head** is considered a holiday delicacy in Norway.

ICE-SKATING MAY HAVE BEEN **INVENTED** 5,000 **YEARS AGO IN FINLAND.**

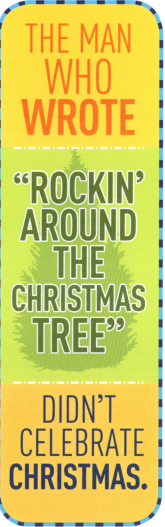

THE MAN WHO WROTE "ROCKIN' AROUND THE CHRISTMAS TREE" DIDN'T CELEBRATE CHRISTMAS.

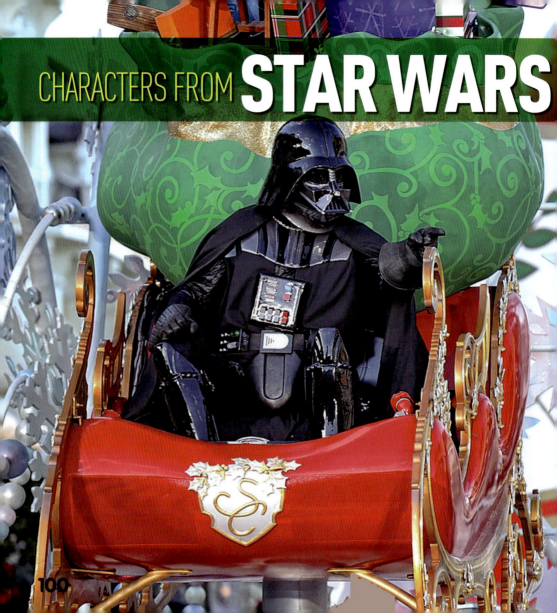

A team in India once constructed **a giant Christmas decoration** as **tall as a 10-story building.**

THE WORLD'S LARGEST CANDY CANE WAS AS LONG AS A GRAY WHALE.

A **mass of sliding snow** can weigh as much as **a million tons.** (907,000 t)

103

RESIDENTS OF SAN DIEGO, CALIFORNIA, U.S.A., FACE A **$250 FINE** IF THEY KEEP THEIR CHRISTMAS LIGHTS UP PAST FEBRUARY 2.

IN THE UNITED STATES ALONE, PEOPLE SPEND MORE THAN **$1 BILLION** EVERY YEAR ON LIVE CHRISTMAS TREES (AND ANOTHER $1.9 BILLION ON FAKE ONES).

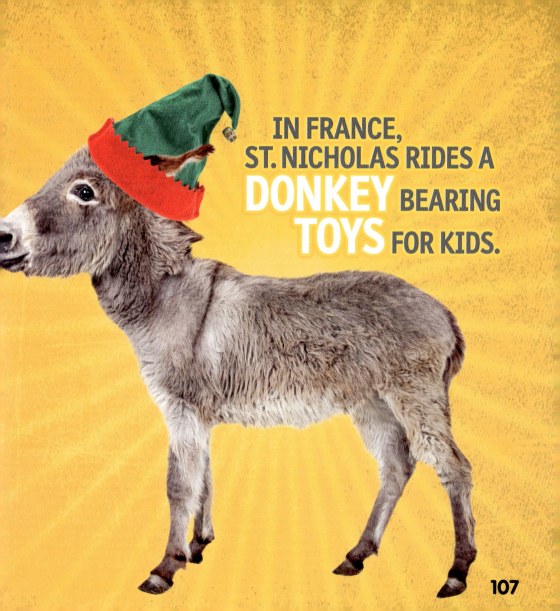

Masked "belsnicklers" go from house to house in parts of Canada asking for treats during the holidays.

IN PARTS OF SPAIN, POPULAR CHRISTMAS DECORATIONS OF PEOPLE USING THE BATHROOM SYMBOLIZE GOOD FORTUNE.

People in Ethiopia, Kazakhstan, Egypt, and Serbia celebrate Christmas on January 7.

A strongman dressed as Santa set a world record by pulling a **17.5-TON** (16-t) "SLEIGH" full of GOODIES down a street in Ontario, Canada.

IN UKRAINE, PEOPLE SCATTER HAY ON THE TABLE AT CHRISTMAS DINNER.

Some of the original British settlers in North America **banned Christmas** *and fined anyone who was found celebrating it.*

IN THE SOUTHERN HEMISPHERE, CHRISTMAS COMES IN THE MIDDLE OF THE SUMMER.

DARTER FISH SPORT RED AND GREEN STRIPES.

A **525-pound** (238-kg) **block of cheese** was once delivered to the mayor of Garland, Texas, U.S.A., as **a Christmas gift.**

BEST PRESENT EVER!

IT TOOK SIX PEOPLE TO HAUL THE CHEESE TO THE MAYOR'S DOOR.

A man dressed as Santa Claus ran the 2015 Philadelphia Marathon in 2 hours 54 seconds.

Hundreds of runners hit the streets of Tokyo, Japan, in **Santa costumes** for the city's annual **Santa Claus Marathon.**

Three brothers in Minnesota, U.S.A., sculpted **A GIANT SEA TURTLE** made of snow that was nearly as tall as their house.

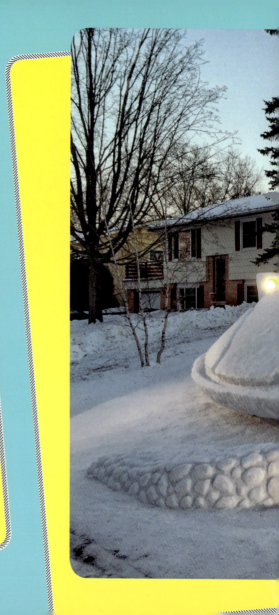

122

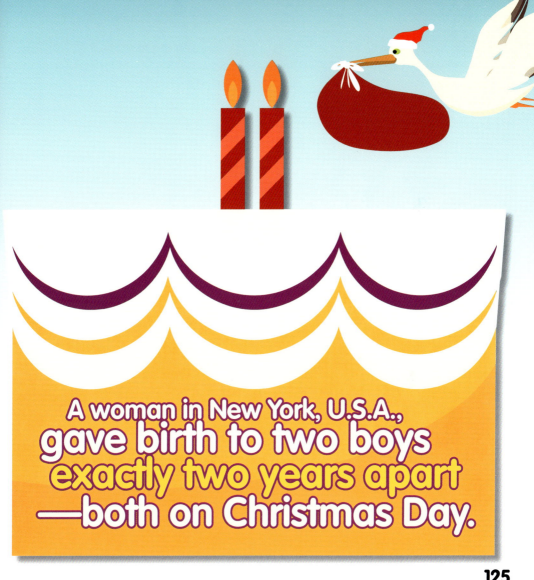

Some people in **BOLIVIA** bring **ROOSTERS** to church on **CHRISTMAS EVE.**

EVERY CHRISTMAS YOU CAN WATCH A BURNING YULE LOG ON TV.

On Christmas Eve in Catalonia, Spain, children hit a hollow log called **TIÓ DE NADAL** with a stick until it "poops" out treats.

When there are no more treats, the log "poops" out garlic or onion.

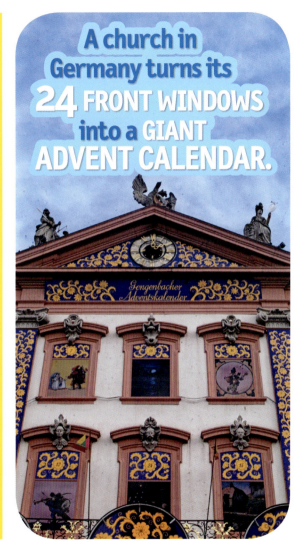

Santa has to cover

150 MILLION MILES
(241 million km)

on his Christmas Eve journey, according to one scientist.

S | M | Tu | W | Th | F

In parts of Belgium, Santa brings presents on December 5

THE AMOUNT OF RIBBON USED TO WRAP GIFTS EACH CHRISTMAS IS ENOUGH TO TIE A BOW AROUND THE ENTIRE PLANET.

A pair of brothers had their picture taken on Santa's lap every year for more than 30 years straight.

137

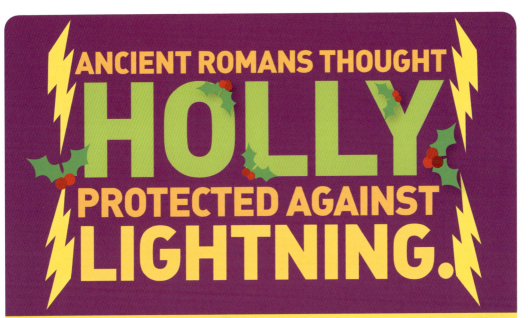

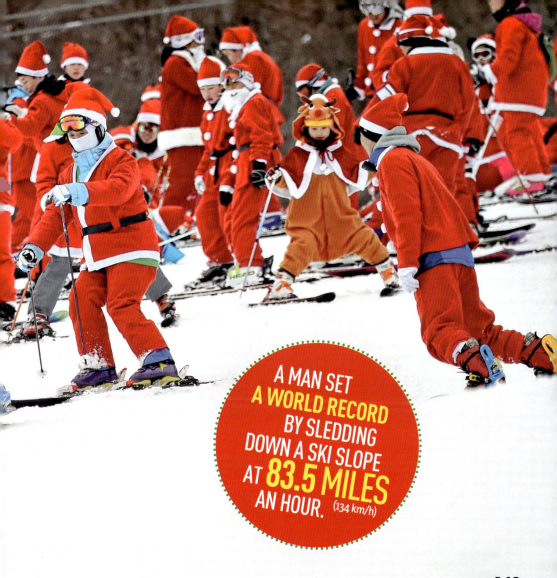

A MAN SET A WORLD RECORD BY SLEDDING DOWN A SKI SLOPE AT 83.5 MILES AN HOUR. (134 km/h)

Each Christmas, Spain hosts the world's largest lottery, with a jackpot of more than $2 billion.

You can buy GINGERBREAD-SCENTED DOG SHAMPOO.

A 10-YEAR-OLD GIRL RECORDED THE HIT SONG "I WANT A HIPPOPOTAMUS FOR CHRISTMAS."

SHE GOT ONE (BUT DONATED IT TO A ZOO).

Hot chocolate was once considered a medicine.

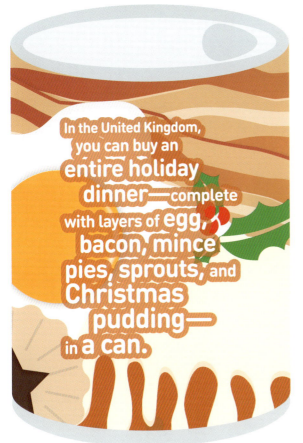

In the United Kingdom, you can buy an **entire holiday dinner**—complete with layers of **egg, bacon, mince pies, sprouts,** and **Christmas pudding**—in **a can.**

Frankincense is sometimes used in toothpaste.

IN MEXICO, CHILDREN CELEBRATE CHRISTMAS BY BREAKING PIÑATAS.

Alabaster Snowball = the name of the elf in charge of

Santa's naughty-or-nice list, according to one tradition.

A NUTCRACKER MUSEUM IN WASHINGTON STATE,

U.S.A., HAS MORE THAN 6,000 NUTCRACKERS.

In medieval Germany, people decorated their Christmas trees with apples, wafers, and cookies.

THE WORLD'S LARGEST SECRET SANTA EXCHANGE INVOLVED 1,463 STUDENTS FROM KENTUCKY, U.S.A.

EARLY COOKIE CUTTERS WERE HANDMADE OUT OF TIN BY LOCAL "TINKERS" — OR TINSMITHS.

IN PIETROȘANI, ROMANIA, VILLAGERS CELEBRATE THE HOLIDAY SEASON BY **RACING HORSES BAREBACK** ACROSS A FIELD.

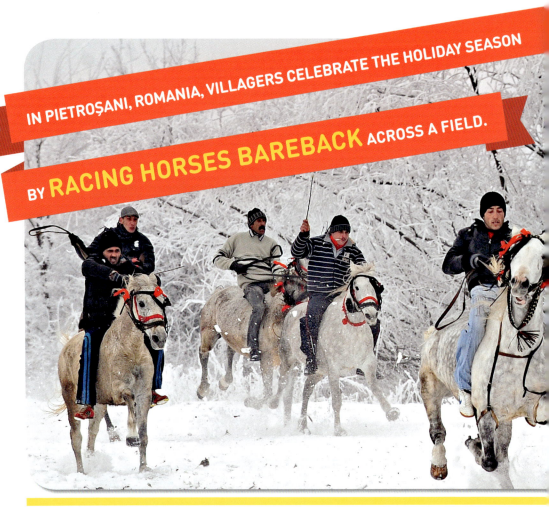

A city in New York State, U.S.A.,

once tried to outlaw snow.

A SHOP IN HOLLYWOOD, CALIFORNIA, U.S.A., SELLS CUSTOM SANTA SUITS FOR UP TO $2,500.

It's a Christmas Eve tradition in Louisiana, U.S.A., to build bonfires on the Mississippi River levees.

Every December, the city of Oslo, Norway, sends the city of London, England, a Christmas tree.

157

U.S. PRESIDENT FRANKLIN DELANO ROOSEVELT RECEIVED A **110-POUND** FRUITCAKE (50-kg) AS A CHRISTMAS GIFT.

ONE FAMILY PASSED DOWN THE SAME FRUITCAKE SINCE **1878.**

AN OREGON, U.S.A., CONGRESSMAN BAKES MORE THAN **200** FRUITCAKES EVERY CHRISTMAS.

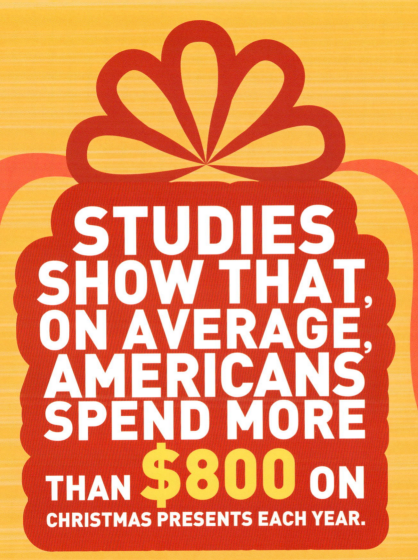

Artificial SNOW can be made out of POTATO STARCH.

Best-selling Christmas toys have included ...

Battery-powered hamsters

A talking stuffed bear

A doll that wets herself

A glowing worm

A team in the Netherlands baked a sweet **CHRISTMAS BREAD** that was nearly as **LONG** as **A CITY BLOCK.**

Some women in medieval Europe **ATE "GINGERBREAD HUSBANDS"** to improve their chances of getting married.

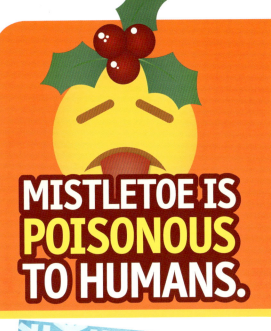

MISTLETOE IS POISONOUS TO HUMANS.

The hook shape of a candy cane is believed to represent a shepherd's staff.

The **2.65 billion Christmas cards** sold each year in the United States could **fill a football field 10 stories high.**

IT TOOK **A MONTH** FOR RESIDENTS IN MAINE, U.S.A., TO BUILD A SNOWWOMAN AS TALL AS **A 12-STORY** BUILDING. IT HAD **SKIS** FOR EYELASHES AND **CAR TIRES** FOR LIPS.

A record-breaking **25,272** carolers gathered together in 2014 to sing Christmas songs in Nigeria, Africa.

MISTLETOE MOTHS lay their **EGGS** on and **FEED** on the popular holiday plant.

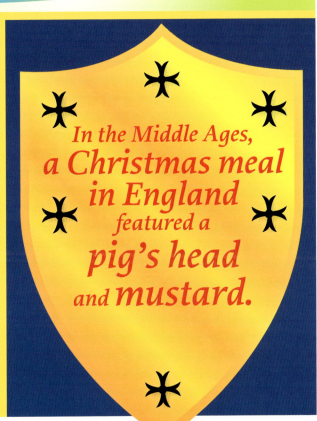

In the Middle Ages, a Christmas meal in England featured a pig's head and mustard.

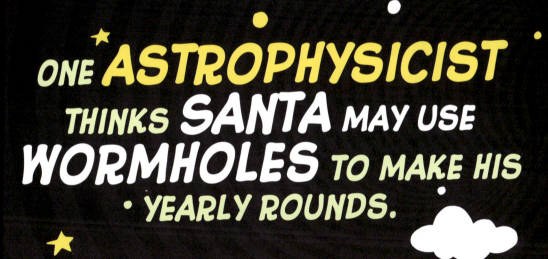

ONE ASTROPHYSICIST THINKS SANTA MAY USE WORMHOLES TO MAKE HIS YEARLY ROUNDS.

SANTA CLAUS CONQUERS THE MARTIANS IS A 1964 MOVIE ABOUT **MARTIANS** WHO COME TO EARTH TO **KIDNAP SANTA.**

BAKERS IN NORWAY MADE A 1,435-POUND (651-kg) GINGERBREAD MAN.

WHEN **WOOD FROGS** HIBERNATE, ABOUT **TWO-THIRDS** OF THEIR BODY'S **WATER** TURNS TO **ICE.**

Eating **peppermint candy** can trick your mouth into feeling cold, research says.

IT'S TRADITION IN GERMANY FOR KIDS TO **LOOK** FOR AN **ORNAMENT** SHAPED LIKE A **PICKLE** HIDDEN ON THE TREE ON CHRISTMAS MORNING.

An estimated **8,200 people** participated in a snowball fight in Saskatchewan, Canada.

Some people think **IT'S BAD LUCK** to take down a Christmas tree before **JANUARY 6.**

In Greece, people EXCHANGE Christmas gifts on JANUARY 1.

AT SOME ZOOS, ELEPHANTS MUNCH ON DISCARDED CHRISTMAS TREES AFTER THE HOLIDAYS.

People have been hanging stockings by fireplaces for more than 400 years.

The **candy cane shrimp** is named for its bright red-and-white striping.

In Guatemala, it's tradition for **JUST THE CHILDREN** to **OPEN PRESENTS ON CHRISTMAS.** (Parents and adults exchange gifts on New Year's Day.)

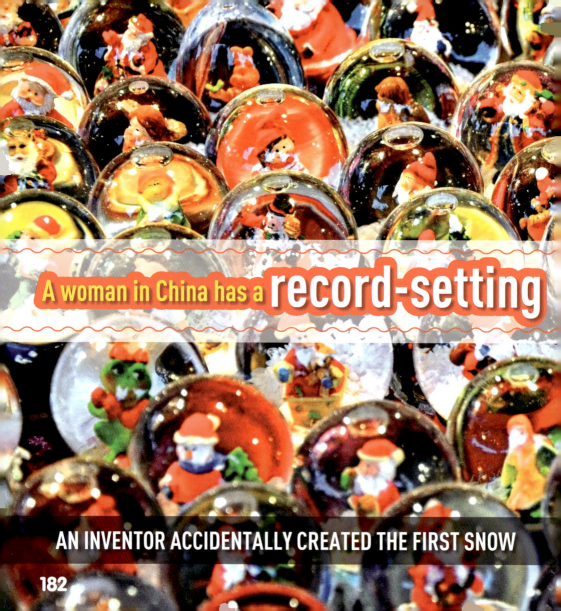

A woman in China has a **record-setting**

AN INVENTOR ACCIDENTALLY CREATED THE FIRST SNOW

182

"Jingle Bells" was not originally written as a Christmas song.

The song's original title? "ONE-HORSE OPEN SLEIGH."

Mistletoe got its name from words meaning "dung on a twig."

A TEAM IN CANADA ONCE BUILT **2,069 SNOWMEN** IN ONE HOUR.

The Maya people boiled poinsettia roots to treat snakebites.

THAT'S WEIRD!

A MAN DRESSED AS SANTA CLAUS WENT SKYDIVING OVER THE NORTH POLE.

HO HO HO!

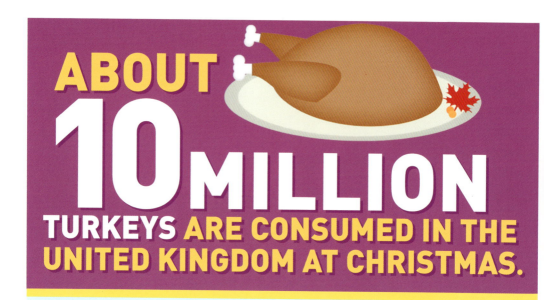

ABOUT **10 MILLION** TURKEYS ARE CONSUMED IN THE UNITED KINGDOM AT CHRISTMAS.

DURING THE U.S. CIVIL WAR, CONFEDERATE TROOPS HAD A 9,000-PERSON SNOWBALL FIGHT.

People used to **dye popcorn bright colors** to string on their Christmas trees.

IN 1836, ALABAMA WAS THE FIRST U.S. STATE TO RECOGNIZE CHRISTMAS AS AN OFFICIAL HOLIDAY.

IN 1907, OKLAHOMA WAS THE LAST U.S. STATE TO RECOGNIZE CHRISTMAS AS AN OFFICIAL HOLIDAY.

CANADA HAS A SPECIAL POST OFFICE FOR LETTERS TO SANTA.

ITS POSTAL CODE IS H0H 0H0.

IT'S TRADITION IN SWEDEN TO WATCH DONALD DUCK CARTOONS ON CHRISTMAS EVE.

THE MYTHICAL KRAMPUS IS SAID TO SWAT NAUGHTY CHILDREN ON CHRISTMAS.

It would cost you more than **$34,000** to buy all the gifts in the song **"THE TWELVE DAYS OF CHRISTMAS."**

A species of snail is named **Ba humbugi**

Families in central Europe traditonally store carp in their bathtubs for a few days before preparing them for Christmas dinner.

FACTFINDER

Boldface indicates illustrations.

A

Advent calendars 132–133, **132–133**
Airplanes 13, **13**
Alabama, U.S.A. 195
Alabaster Snowball (elf) 146–147
Alternate days for Christmas 109, 137, 176, 179
Ancient Romans 139
Animal crackers 70, **70**
Animals, talking 187, **187**
Artificial Christmas trees 63, **63,** 106, 137, **137**
Artificial snow 72, **72,** 161
Astronauts *see* Space travel
Australia 113, 180, 181

B

Ba humbugi (snail) 198
Banana trees 11
Bans on Christmas 114
Bathtubs, carp in 198, **198**
Bauble ornaments 5, **5**
Bears 2, **2**
Beetles 181, **181**
Befana (witch) 16
Belgium 137
Belsnicklers (Canadian tradition) 109
Bethlehem, Star of 57, **57**

Birthdays, on Christmas 125, 138
Blitzen (reindeer) 10, **10**
Bolivia 129
Bonfires 157, **157**
Bows, on buildings 38, **38**
Brazil 39
Bread, Christmas 162, **162**
Britain *see* England; United Kingdom

C

Canada
  belsnicklers 109
  post office for letters to Santa 197
  skiers dressed as Santa or Mrs. Claus 140, **140–141**
  snowball fight 176
  snowmen 185
Candy
  chocolate 98, **98**
  on Christmas lists 170, **170, 171**
  peppermint 172, **172**
  see also Candy canes
Candy cane shrimp 179, **179**
Candy canes
  eating methods 35, **35**
  flavors 26, 196, **196**
  largest 103
  National Candy Cane Day 71, **71**
  original shape and color 28, **28**
  shape 28, **28,** 163, **163**

Canned Christmas dinner 145, **145**
Caracas, Venezuela 65
Carp, in bathtubs 198, **198**
Catalonia, Spain 130, **130–131**
Cats 192, **192–193**
Cheese 118, **118**
"Chestnuts Roasting on an Open Fire" (song) 9
Chicken, fried 71, **71**
Chickens, in church 129, **129**
Chile 86
Chocolate 98, **98**
Christmas
  alternate days for 109, 137, 176, 179
  bans on 114
  as official holiday 195
Christmas, Michigan, U.S.A. 47
Christmas beetles 181, **181**
Christmas bread 162, **162**
Christmas cards
  auction price 33, **33**
  number sold each year 163
  from pets 192
  sent to strangers 175
  tiny 76
Christmas carols *see* Songs and carols
Christmas lights
  candles 37
  fines for 106, **106**
  first 134, **134**
  recycled 43, **43**

Rockefeller Center 160, **160**
seen from space 139, **139**
Christmas lists 8, 170
Christmas pudding 51, 113, 145
"The Christmas Song (Chestnuts Roasting on an Open Fire)" 9
Christmas trees
animal cracker decorations 70, **70**
artificial 63, **63,** 106, 138, **138**
banana trees as 11, **11**
candles on 37, **37**
chopping record 29
cloned 52, **52**
dog poo ornament 191, **191**
early decorations 58
edible **6–7,** 7
farm-grown 15, **15**
food decorations 70, **70,** 152, 195
giant bauble ornament 5, **5**
gifting 157
growing 98, **98**
jewelry decorations 49, **49**
number of species 135
pickle ornaments 174, **174**
popcorn on 195
Rockefeller Center 124, **124,** 160, **160**
in space 96–97, **96–97**
spending on 106
stealing 150–151
taking down, date for 176, **176**

tallest living 68, **68–69**
tinsel 58, **58**
upside-down 108, **108,** 138, **138**
uses for old ones 21, **21,** 27, **27,** 178
in the White House 28, 36
Christmas trees worms 104–105, **104–105**
Civil War, U.S.A. 190
Claus, Mrs. 140, **140–141**
Claus, Santa *see* Santa Claus
Cloned Christmas trees 52, **52**
Coconut eggnog 177, **177**
Cook County, Illinois, U.S.A. 27
Cookies
cookie cutters 153
as decorations 194, **194**
gingerbread men **74–75,** 75, 82, **82,** 163, 171, **171**

D

Darter fish 115, **115**
Darth Vader **100–101**
Decorations
giant 103
people using the bathroom 109
radishes **94**
see also Christmas trees
Denmark 86
Detroit, Michigan, U.S.A. 23
Diamonds, in Advent calendar 133, **133**

Dog poo ornament 191, **191**
Dogs 143, 192–193, **192–193**
Donald Duck cartoons 197
Donkeys 107, **107**
Donner (reindeer) 10, **10**
Druids 77

E

Edison, Thomas 134, **134**
Eels **24–25,** 25
Eggnog 177, **177**
Eggnog, Utah, U.S.A. 46
Eggnog-flavored lip balm 11, **11**
Egypt 109
Elephants **78,** 178
Elf Training Academy, Finland 102
Elizabeth I, Queen (England) 82
Elves 23, **23, 54–55,** 55, 102, **102,** 146–147
England
Christmas trees 157
jumping in icy water 102, **102**
life-size gingerbread cookies 82, **82**
Middle Ages 165
see also United Kingdom
Ethiopia 109

F

Finland 99, 102
Fish 115, **115,** 198, **198**

201

FACTFINDER

Florida, U.S.A. 84, **84–85**
Food
   candy 98, **98**, 170, **170**, **171**,
     172, **172**
   candy canes 26, 71, **71**, 103, 163,
     163, 196, **196**
   canned holiday dinner 145,
     145
   carp 198, **198**
   caterpillars 11, **11**
   cheese 118, **118**
   chocolate 98, **98**
   Christmas bread 162, **162**
   Christmas pudding 51, 113, 145
   desserts with inedible items
     49, **49**
   eggnog 177, **177**
   fried chicken 71, **71**
   fruitcake 58, 158, **158**
   gingerbread houses 40–41,
     40–41
   gingerbread men **74–75**, 75,
     82, **82**, 163, 171, **171**
   hot chocolate 79, **79**, 145, 199,
     199
   medieval times 45
   mince pie 52
   nuts 170, **170**
   oranges 189, **189**
   pig's heads 165
   pudding 51, 113
   radishes **94**

   sheep's head 99
   sugarplums 16, **16**
   Tudor Christmas pie 79, **79**
   turkeys 190, **190**
Fox urine 151
France 86, 107
Frankincense 145
Frogs 172, **172**
Fruitcake 58, 158, **158**

G

Gävle, Sweden 92, **92–93**
Germany 133, 135, 152, 174
Ghost stories 37
Gifts
   for pets 193, **193**
   re-gifting 173, **173**
   spending on 159
   wrapping 137, 138
   wrapping paper 32–33, **32–33**
Gingerbread houses 40–41,
   40–41
Gingerbread men **74–75**, 75, 82,
   82, 163, 171, **171**
Gingerbread-scented dog
   shampoo 143
Goats 56, **56**, 92, **92–93**
Goblins 147, **147**
Gold, in Christmas pudding 113
"Good King Wenceslas" (song) 28
Greece 147, 176, **176**
Guatemala 179

H

Hawaii, U.S.A. 126, **126–127**
Hay, as decoration 114
Hippopotamuses **50**, 143, **143**
Holly 139, **139**
Horseback riding 154, **154–155**
Hot chocolate 79, **79**, 145, 199,
   199

I

"I Want a Hippopotamus for
   Christmas" (song) 143
Ice 76
Ice-skating **30–31**, 31, 99, **99**
Iceland 62, 116, **116**, 117
Icicles 4, 9, 20, **20**
Icy water, jumping in 102, **102**
Idaho, U.S.A. 68
India 11, 103
International University of
   Santa Claus 27, **27**
Italy 16
It's a Wonderful Life (movie)
   72, **72**

J

Jackson, Andrew 73
Japan 71, 80
Jesus 29, 57
Jewelry, as ornaments 49, **49**
"Jingle Bells" (song) 43, 184
Jolly, Texas, U.S.A. 46

202

K

Kallikantzaroi (goblins) 147, **147**
Kazakhstan 109
Kentucky, U.S.A. 152
Krampus (mythical creature) 197

L

Legs (branches of icicles) 20, **20**
"Let It Snow!" (song) 37
Lip balm 11, **11**
London, England 157
Lotteries 142
Louisiana, U.S.A. 157

M

Map, Christmas place-names 46–47
Marathons **74–75,** 75, 119, **120– 121,** 121
Martians 168, **168–169**
Maryland, U.S.A. 87
Maya 185
Mexico 146, 199
Minnesota, U.S.A. 122, **122–123**
Mistletoe
  exploding 9
  meaning of name 185
  number of species 38
  as poisonous 163, **163**
  as witchcraft protection 77
Mistletoe, Kentucky, U.S.A. 47
Mistletoe moths 165, **165**

Moctezuma II, Emperor (Mexico) 199
Moray eels **24–25,** 25
Moths 165, **165**
Mrs. Claus 140, **140–141**

N

NASA *see* Space travel
National Candy Cane Day 71
Naughty children 117, 197
Naughty-or-nice list 146–147
Netherlands 162, **162**
Nigeria 165
North Pole 42, **42,** 73, 188
North Pole, Alaska, U.S.A. 46, 90
Norway 36, 99, 157, 171, **171**
The Nutcracker (ballet) 44
Nutcracker museum, Washington State, U.S.A. 148–149, **148–149**

O

"O Christmas Tree" (song) 87
Oklahoma, U.S.A. 195
Oranges 189, **189**
Ornaments *see* Christmas trees
Oslo, Norway 157
Owls **110–111,** 111

P

Paper snowflakes 166, **166**
Pennsylvania Dutch 194

Peppermint candy 172, **172,** 196, **196**
Peru 199
Pets 192–193, **192–193**
Philadelphia Marathon 119
Pickle ornaments 174, **174**
Pierce, Franklin 36, **36**
Pietroșani, Romania 154
Pig's head, as food 165
Piñatas 146, **146**
Place-names 46–47
Poinsettias 26–27, **26–27,** 70, **70,** 185
Polar bears 2, **2**
Poop 130, **130–131,** 191, **191**
Popcorn 195, **195**
Presents
  for pets 193, **193**
  re-gifting 173, **173**
  spending on 159
  wrapping 137, 138
  wrapping paper 32–33, **32–33**
Puerto Rico 177

R

Re-gifting 173, **173**
Reindeer **60–61**
  antlers 12, **12,** 60
  facts 60–61
  migration 156, **156**
  names 10, **10,** 64
Ribbon 137, **137**

203

FACTFINDER

Rockefeller Center, New York City, U.S.A. 124, **124**, 160, **160**
"Rockin' Around the Christmas Tree" (song) 99
Roller-skating 65, **65**
Romania 154
Romans, ancient 139
Roosevelt, Franklin Delano 158
Roosevelt, Theodore 28, **28**
Roosters 129, **129**
Rudolph (reindeer) 64

S

Saint Nicholas *see* Santa Claus
Sandmen 84, **84–85**
Santa Claus (St. Nicholas)
    alternate transportation 107, 126, **126–127**, 180
    chocolate 98, **98**
    collection of 45
    custom suits 157, **157**
    distance traveled 136
    elected official 90
    gifts in shoes 135, **135**
    government tracking 18, **18**
    hats 59, **59**
    kidnapped by Martians 168, **168–169**
    letters in Canada 197
    mall Santa school 27, **27**
    marathons 119, **120–121**, 121
    names for 14
    number of stops 35
    pictures with 137
    skiing 140, **140–141**
    skydiving 188, **188**
    speed of travel 39, 95, 186, **186**
    strongman 112, **112**
    treats left for 86, **86**
    wealth 4, **4**
    wormholes, use of 167
    Yule Lads 116, **116**, 117
Santa Claus, Georgia, U.S.A. 47
Santa Claus Conquers the Martians (movie) 168, **168–169**
Saskatchewan, Canada 176
Sea turtles, from snow 122, **122–123**
Secret Santa exchanges 152
Serbia 109
Shampoo, gingerbread-scented 143
Sheep's head, as food 99
Shoes, gifts in 117, **117**, 135, **135**
Shopping
    amount spent 32
    amount spent on candy 98
    amount spent on presents 159
    amount spent on wrapping paper 32–33
    predictions 53
    speed of checkout lines 66
    store music 32
    time spent 39
Shrimp 179, **179**
Silver Bell, Arizona, U.S.A. 46
Skiing 140–141, **140–141**
Skunk scent 150
Skydiving 188, **188**
Sleds and toboggans 13, 49
Snails 198
Snakebites, poinsettia for 185
Snow
    absorbing sound waves 48
    artificial 72, **72**, 161
    blue 34
    mazes 88, **88–89**
    outlawed 154–155
    paper snowflakes 166, **166**
    permanent coverage 76
    sculptures 122, **122–123**
    snow angels 128, **128**
    snowball fights 73, 176, 190
    snowflakes 17, **17**, 22, **22**, 82, **82**
    snowstorms 63, **63**
    weight 103
    white lightning 91, **91**
Snow globes 182–183, **182–183**
Snowflake moray eels **24–25**, 25
Snowmen
    chocolate 98, **98**
    exploding 67, **67**
    giant 164, **164**
    ideal temperature 144, **144**
    number built at ice festival 80, **80–81**
    number built in one hour 185
    from sand 84, **85**
Snowy owls **110–111**, 111

204

Songs and carols
"The Christmas Song (Chestnuts Roasting on an Open Fire)" 9
"Good King Wenceslas" 28
highest-altitude concert 13
"I Want a Hippopotamus for Christmas" 143
"Jingle Bells" 43, 184
"Let It Snow!" 37
"O Christmas Tree" 87
origin of caroling 73
"Rockin' Around the Christmas Tree" 99
"The Twelve Days of Christmas" 64, 198
world records 165
Sound waves 48
South Africa 11
Southern Hemisphere 115
Space travel
Christmas carols 43
Christmas lights seen during 139, **139**
Christmas trees 96–97, **96–97**
pranks 19, **19**
Spain 109, 130, **130–131**, 142
Spiders 79
St. Nicholas *See* Santa Claus
Stars 57, **57**
Stockings 76, **76**, 178, **178**, 189, **189**
Sugarplums 16, **16**

Supernovas 57, **57**
Sweaters 83, **83**
Sweden 86, 92, **92–93**, 197
Switzerland 67

T

Television, Yule log on 129, **129**
Tió de Nadal 130, **130–131**
Toboggans and sleds 13, 49
Tokyo, Japan **120–121**, 121
Tongue, stuck on frozen metal 4, **4**
Toothpaste, frankincense in 145, **145**
Towns with holiday names 46–47
Toys, best-selling 161
Tudor Christmas pie 79, **79**
Turkeys 190, **190**
Turtles, from snow 122, **122–123**
TV, Yule log on 129, **129**
Twelve days of Christmas (tradition) 45, 52, 147
"The Twelve Days of Christmas" (song) 64, 198

U

Ukraine 79, 114
United Kingdom
canned Christmas dinner 145, **145**
Christmas desserts 49
Christmas turkeys 190, **190**
mince pie 52

treats for Santa 86, **86**
see also England
United States
Christmas place-names 46–47
Civil War snowball fight 190
treats for Santa 86, **86**

V

Venezuela 65
Vikings 49, **49**

W

Washington State, U.S.A. 148–149
Wassailing 73
Wenceslas, King (Bohemia) 28
Whale bones, toboggans from 13
White House, Washington, D.C., U.S.A. 28, 36, 73, 166
White lightning 91, **91**
Witches 16, 36, 77
Wood frogs 172, **172**
Wormholes 167
Worms, Christmas tree 104–105, **104–105**
Wrapping paper 32–33, **32–33**
Wreath, world's largest 78

Y

Yule Cat 62, **62**
Yule Doo (ornament) 191, **191**
Yule goat 92, **92–93**
Yule Lads 116, **116**, 117
Yule logs 129, **129**

Copyright © 2017 National Geographic Partners, LLC

All rights reserved. Reproduction of the whole or any part of the contents without written permission from the publisher is prohibited.

NATIONAL GEOGRAPHIC and Yellow Border Design are trademarks of the National Geographic Society, used under license.

Since 1888, the National Geographic Society has funded more than 14,000 research, conservation, education, and storytelling projects around the world. National Geographic Partners distributes a portion of the funds it receives from your purchase to National Geographic Society to support programs including the conservation of animals and their habitats. To learn more, visit natgeo.com/info.

For more information, visit nationalgeographic.com, call 1-877-873-6846, or write to the following address:

National Geographic Partners, LLC
1145 17th Street NW
Washington, DC 20036-4688 U.S.A.

More for kids from National Geographic:
natgeokids.com

National Geographic Kids magazine inspires children to explore their world with fun yet educational articles on animals, science, nature, and more. Using fresh storytelling and amazing photography, *Nat Geo Kids* shows kids ages 6 to 14 the fascinating truth about the world—and why they should care.
natgeo.com/subscribe

For rights or permissions inquiries, please contact National Geographic Books Subsidiary Rights: bookrights@natgeo.com

Designed by Julide Dengel

The publisher would like to thank Avery Hurt, author and researcher; Sarah Wassner Flynn, author and researcher; Jen Agresta, project manager; Paige Towler, project editor; Hillary Leo of Royal Scruff, photo editor; Lori Epstein, photo director; Alix Inchausti, production editor; and Anne LeongSon, design production assistant.

Title: Weird but true Christmas / by National Geographic Kids.
Other titles: National Geographic kids.
Description: Washington, DC : National Geographic Kids, [2017] | Series: Weird but true | Includes index. | Audience: Ages: 8-12. | Audience: Grades: 4 to 6.
Identifiers: LCCN 2017010392| ISBN 9781426328893 (paperback : alk. paper) | ISBN 9781426328909 (hardcover)
Subjects: LCSH: Christmas--Juvenile literature.
Classification: LCC GT4985.5 .W47 2017 | DDC 263/.915--dc23
LC record available at https://lccn.loc.gov /2017010392

Printed in South Korea
24/ISK/7 (SC)
24/ISK/3 (RLB)

206

PHOTO CREDITS

All artwork by MODUZA DESIGN and Julide Dengel unless otherwise noted below.

FRONT COVER: (polar bear), Eric Isselee/GlobalP/iStockphoto/Getty Images; (elf hat), Leslie Banks/iStockphoto/Getty Images; (candy cane), photastic/Shutterstock; (gold glitter), surachet khamsuk/Shutterstock; (silver glitter), rangizzz/Shutterstock; **SPINE:** (polar bear), Eric Isselee/GlobalP/iStockphoto/Getty Images; (elf hat), Leslie Banks/iStockphoto/Getty Images; **BACK COVER:** (bells), indigolotos/Shutterstock

INTERIOR: 2 (UP), Leslie Banks/iStockphoto/Getty Images; 2 (LO), Eric Isselee/GlobalP/iStockphoto/Getty Images; 4 (LE), Larry Williams/Getty Images; 4 (CTR), Ljupco Smokovski/Shutterstock; 4 (RT back), surachet khamsuk/Shutterstock; 6-7, Nature Picture Library/Alamy Stock Photo; 11, iStockphoto/Getty Images; 13, ifong/Shutterstock; 14, gillmar/Shutterstock; 16, Tim Hill/Alamy Stock Photo; 19 (CTR), abramsdesign/Shutterstock; 19 (UP), Lizavetta/Shutterstock; 19 (LO), stockphoto/Shutterstock; 20, Tiplyashina/Shutterstock; 22, Alexey Kljatov/Shutterstock; 24, imageBROKER RM/Getty Images; 26-27 (LO), ND700/Shutterstock; 27, PA Images/Alamy Stock Photo; 28 (LE), Library of Congress Prints and Photographs Division; 28 (RT), Shade Studios/Shutterstock; 29 (UP), Barbol/Shutterstock; 29 (LO), Manfred Ruckszio/Shutterstock; 30-31, Brad Kitching; 32 (UP), Fat Jackey/Shutterstock; 32 (LO), Sandra Cunningham/Shutterstock; 33 (UP), courtesy Henry Aldridge & Son; 34, Mike Theiss/National Geographic Creative; 36, Corbis/Getty Images; 38 (UP), Ringo Chiu/ZUMAPRESS/Alamy Stock Photo; 38 (LO), Valentina Razumova/Shutterstock; 39, Neirfy/Shutterstock; 39 (LE), Golubovy/Shutterstock; 40-41, WENN/Newscom; 40-41, loskutnikov/Shutterstock; 42, Sue Flood/NPL/Minden Pictures; 43, David Aguilar; 45, Thinkstock; 49 (UP LE), AFP/Getty Images; 49 (UP CTR LE), Picsfive/Shutterstock; 49 (UP CTR RT), Sean Locke Photography/Shutterstock; 49 (UP RT), indigolotos/Shutterstock; 49 (LO), iStockphoto/Getty Images; 50, tratong/Shutterstock; 50 (UP), gillmar/Shutterstock; 54, EPA/Newscom; 57, Ikon Images/Getty Images; 59, © Icon Sports Media Inc./Newscom; 58, Kamenetskiy Konstantin/Shutterstock; 60, Dmitry Chulov/Shutterstock; 63, iStockphoto/Getty Images; 67 (LE), iStockphoto/Getty Images; 67 (RT), iStockphoto/Getty Images; 68, courtesy Coure d'Alene Resort/Blue 541 Marketing; 70 (RT), Reshavskyi/Shutterstock; 70 (RT insets), Bill Truran/Alamy Stock Photo; 72 (LE), Martha Holmes/The LIFE Picture Collection/Getty Image; 72 (RT), AF archive/Alamy Stock Photo; 73, Pixel 4 Images/Shutterstock; 74-75, Jeremy Pembrey/Alamy Stock Photo; 78, abadonian/iStockphoto; 78 (UP), gillmar/Shutterstock; 79 (LE), iStockphoto/Getty Images; 79 (RT), Rob Hainer/Shutterstock; 79 (RT inset), Alex Staroseltsev/Shutterstock; 80, © 2008 Christopher Chan/Getty Images; 82, Ruth Black/Shutterstock; 83, Tribune News Service/Getty Images; 84, iStockphoto/Getty Images; 86 (UP LE), maryskin/AdobeStock; 86, Subbotina Anna/Shutterstock; 86 (UP RT), margouillat photo/Shutterstock; 86 (LO LE), Leigh Prather/Shutterstock; 86 (LO CTR), NinjaTaTaa/Shutterstock; 86, Liljam/Shutterstock; 88, courtesy Fort William Historical Park; 91, Creative Travel Projects/Shutterstock; 93, Anders Tukler/Alamy Stock Photo; 94, Judith Haden/Danita Delimont/Newscom; 96, NASA; 98, claire norman/Shutterstock; 99, Shutterstock; 100, Getty Images; 102, Dimitris Legakis/Splash News/Newscom; 103, PHOTOCREO Michal Bednarek/Shutterstock; 104, OceanPhoto/FLPA/Minden Pictures; 107 (LO), Rosa Jay/Shutterstock; 107 (UP), iStockphoto/Getty Images; 110, FotoRequest/Shutterstock; 112, TIGG Media/WENN/Newscom; 114 (LE), Nattawat Kaewjirasit/Shutterstock; 114 (RT), abramsdesign/Shutterstock; 115, Joel Sartore/National Geographic Creative; 116, Arctic Images/Alamy Stock Photo; 117 (UP LE), Hong Vo/Shutterstock; 117 (CTR), schab/Shutterstock; 117 (UP RT), cristovao/Shutterstock; 118, fotoret/Shutterstock; 120, Yoshikazu Tsuno/AFP/Getty Images; 122, Bartz Snow Sculptures; 124, Gilbert Carrasquillo/FilmMagic/Getty Images; 126, Chilkoot/Dreamstime; 128, Shutterstock; 129, PCHT/Shutterstock; 130, Natali Zakharova/Shutterstock; 130 (LE), Nik Merkulov/Shutterstock; 132, courtesy The Green Space; 133 (LE), © Octagon Blue/Solent News; 133 (RT), Peter Bischoff/Getty Images; 134 (back), Mondadori Portfolio/Getty Images; 134 (LE), Danno333/Dreamstime; 135, Nicole Gordine/Shutterstock; 137, Fisherss/Shutterstock; 139, NASA; 140, The Asahi Shimbun/Getty Images; 143, JStaley401/Shutterstock; 144, Smit/Shutterstock; 146, Graffizone/iStockphoto; 148, Koi88/Dreamstime; 150, Eric Isselee/Shutterstock; 151, Eric Isselee/Shutterstock; 152, © 2011 Krista Long/Getty Images; 153, Mliberra/Shutterstock; 154, AFP/Getty Images; 156, Michio Hoshino/Minden Pictures; 158, EM Arts/Shutterstock; 160, JStone/Shutterstock; 162, AP Photo/Stephanie Pilick/picture-alliance/dpa; 165, iStockphoto/Getty Images; 166, © Ej Hersom/Planet Pix via ZUMA Wire/Newscom; 168, Courtesy Everett Collection; 171, AP Photo/Morten Holm/Scanpix; 172, Joel Sartore, National Geographic Photo Ark/National Geographic Creative; 173 (UP), AlexeiLogvinovich/Shutterstock; 173 (LO), Alexei Logvinovich/Shutterstock; 174, iStockphoto/Getty Images; 176, kwest/Shutterstock; 179, Franco Banfi/Biosphoto/Minden Pictures; 181, Rob Walls/Alamy Stock Photo; 182, Koi88/Dreamstime; 185, kamnuan/Shutterstock; 186 (back), ESA/Hubble & NASA; 187, Annette Shaff/Shutterstock; 188, Mauricio Graiki/Shutterstock; 192, Liliya Kulianionak/Shutterstock; 196, iStockphoto; 197, Nicescene/Shutterstock; 198, lendy16/Shutterstock; 198 (LO), Vadym Zaitsev/Shutterstock

30 WONDERFUL WAYS TO SAY THANKS!

Friends! Family! Teachers! Neighbors! There are plenty of awesome people to thank and reasons to be thankful throughout the year, and this book can help you do so.

FIND INSIDE!
30 PULL-OUT THANK-YOU CARDS featuring adorable animals and funny sayings!

AVAILABLE WHEREVER BOOKS ARE SOLD
Get a fun freebie at natgeokids.com/fun-pack

© 2017 National Geographic Partners, LLC